101

Annoying Things

About Other Drivers

Ray Comfort

First Printing: March 2007

Copyright © 2007 by Ray Comfort. All rights reserved. No part of this
book may be used or reproduced in any manner whatsoever without
written permission of the publisher except in the case of brief quotations
in articles and reviews. For information write: New Leaf Press, P.O. Box
726, Green Forest, AR 72638.

ISBN-13: 978-0-89221-668-0
ISBN-10: 0-89221-668-9
Library of Congress Catalog Number: 2006937544
Cover design by Janell Robertson.

Printed in the United States of America.

New Leaf Press
A Division of New Leaf Publishing Group

Drivers who try and suffocate you with their exhaust fumes.

Tailgaters who act like they're trying to dock with the Enterprise.

IF AT FIRST YOU DON'T SUCCEED, DON'T TRY SKYDIVING.

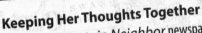

Keeping Her Thoughts Together

The *Ouachita Mountain Neighbor* newspaper in Arkansas reported the following incident on September 26, 1995:

A local woman in a small town came out of a Wal-Mart store, placed her groceries in the back of her car, and sat in the driver's seat.

Suddenly, she heard what sounded like a loud gunshot crashing through her back window, and in the same instant something impacted the back of her head.

Terrified, she put her hand on the back of her head and felt the horrific sensation of her warm brains oozing onto her hand. She screamed in terror and went into a fit of uncontrollable hysterics.

A number of frantic shoppers immediately called 911 on their cellular phones, and within minutes police arrived and rushed to the aid of the screaming woman.

It was then that an officer of the law leaned into the vehicle. After hearing that the woman was literally holding her brains in, he gently pried her hand from the back of her head and found some gooey, warm biscuit dough. The woman had purchased a can of the mixture with her groceries, left it in the hot sun, and it had expanded and exploded with a bang, sending warm dough onto the back of her head.

"I drive with my knees. Otherwise, how can I put on my lipstick and talk on the phone?" – Sharon Stone

Slow drivers who speed up when you try and overtake them.

TIME IS WHAT KEEPS THINGS FROM HAPPENING ALL AT ONCE.

Slow drivers who cross into the lane you just moved to so you could get away from them.

Drivers whose bumper stickers are too small to read (without tailgating).

"It takes 8,460 bolts to assemble an automobile, and one nut to scatter it all over the road." — *Author Unknown*

LOTTERY: A TAX ON PEOPLE WHO ARE BAD AT MATH.

Slow cars in the fast lane.

Fast cars in the slow lane.

IT'S LONELY AT THE TOP,
BUT YOU EAT BETTER.

Drivers who take two seconds to cross six lanes to exit the freeway.

After Her Own Kind

My mom (who takes after me) pulled in behind two cars and waited patiently to turn into a one-way street. After some time she realized the cars didn't have drivers. They weren't waiting to go around the corner — they were *parked* on the side of the road.

I DON'T SUFFER FROM INSANITY,
I ENJOY EVERY MINUTE OF IT.

Drivers whose trucks are two miles high, who don't care if they crush you against the freeway wall.

People who don't use turning signals.

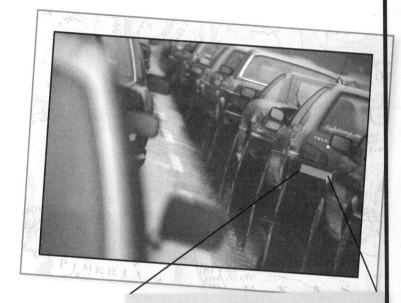

NEVER ANSWER AN ANONYMOUS LETTER.

Big Mouth

I was waiting to be picked up by a man to be taken to a meeting. The friend I was staying with said, "The first thing you will notice about Chuck is his big nose." His wife chided him for such talk, but he insisted, "I'm serious. The poor man's nose is *huge*." I said, "Thanks a lot. The first thing I will see is his nose, and I don't want to embarrass the man, so let's not talk about that subject any more."

That didn't quiet down my twisted buddy. He must have mentioned that man's nose another three or four times. Of course, knowing that he had a twisted sense of humor, I took what he was saying with a large pinch of salt. About an hour later, we were waiting outside for Chuck to pick me up for the meeting and I was a little concerned as to whether or not he would have room in his car for eight boxes of my books and tapes.

When he was late, my warped companion said, "I don't know what could have happened to him — he *nose* where to come."

I ignored him. I wanted to be a kind, loving, caring, and warm person, and would rather die than make fun of another person's physical appearance.

Suddenly, he came around the corner in a *very small* car. As we were introduced (for some reason), I couldn't help but notice his nose. It was generous, but my friend had been exaggerating a little.

The last thing in the world I wanted to do was to draw attention to it, so I looked at my eight boxes and casually said, *"I hope you have a big trunk!"* As my friend and I stuck our heads into the trunk to arrange the boxes, he choked out, *"How could you say such a thing!"*

He's probably telling someone right now about the size of my big mouth.

Drivers who back their vehicles out of the driveway onto the road, *then* look to see if anything is coming.

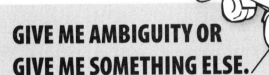

GIVE ME AMBIGUITY OR GIVE ME SOMETHING ELSE.

Horn honkers who honk at nothing and scare the living daylights out of you.

Truckers whose tires send out so much spray on a rainy day you can't see your windshield.

FORGET ABOUT WORLD PEACE...
VISUALIZE USING YOUR TURN SIGNAL.

"The best car safety device is a rear-view mirror with a cop in it." — Dudley Moore

Drivers who drive two inches from a freeway wall.

WE HAVE ENOUGH YOUTH. HOW ABOUT A FOUNTAIN OF "SMART"?

"You know, somebody actually complimented me on my driving today. They left a little note on the windscreen, it said 'Parking Fine.'"
– Tommy Cooper

Drivers who refuse to slow down to 140 mph in the rain.

Drivers who insist on having eye contact with you as you sit in the back seat of their car.

CAMPERS: NATURE'S WAY OF FEEDING MOSQUITOES.

THREE KINDS OF PEOPLE: THOSE WHO CAN COUNT AND THOSE WHO CAN'T.

People who treat their brake pedal like the drum pedal in a rap song.

Give Me a Brake

In April 1970, a Mrs. Miriam Hargrave set a new world record. As she drove through a set of red lights, she failed her driving test, bringing it to a total of 39 failed tests. In the preceding eight years, she had received over 200 driving lessons. Trailing far behind her was an unnamed woman from Auburn, California, who failed her driving test in the first second. She got into the car, said, "Good morning" to the tester, started the engine, and shot straight through the wall of the Driving Test Center. She mistook the accelerator for the clutch.

18

Drivers who enter a freeway
at a dead snail's pace.

19

People who refuse to
make room for you as
you enter a freeway.

CONSCIOUSNESS: THAT ANNOYING TIME BETWEEN NAPS.

Spilled Milk

In Benton, Arkansas, two men were crying over spilled milk when they broke out of the county jail and stole a milk truck as a getaway vehicle. However, they left the back door of the truck open, spewing cartons of milk onto the road behind them, leaving a milk trail for the local sheriff to follow. He apprehended them about 30 miles from the jail.

Drivers who hide behind dark windows.

"Living on earth may be expensive, but it includes an annual free trip around the sun." – Anonymous

WHY IS "ABBREVIATION" SUCH A LONG WORD?

Rubberneckers.

Drivers who don't slow down enough for you to rubber-neck.

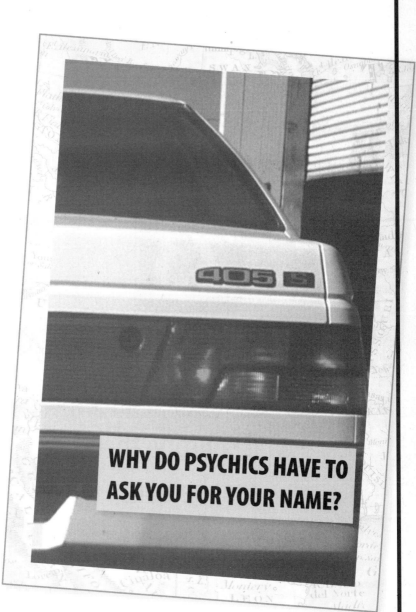

Oncoming drivers who
drive with their knees,
while putting their
seat belt on.

CHANGE IS INEVITABLE, EXCEPT FROM A VENDING MACHINE.

"Have you ever noticed that anybody driving slower than you is an idiot, and anyone going faster than you is a maniac?" – George Carlin

Oncoming drivers who put on lipstick while driving.

Drivers who comb their hair while driving.

COVER ME. I'M CHANGING LANES.

26

Drivers whose kids don't
wear seat belts.

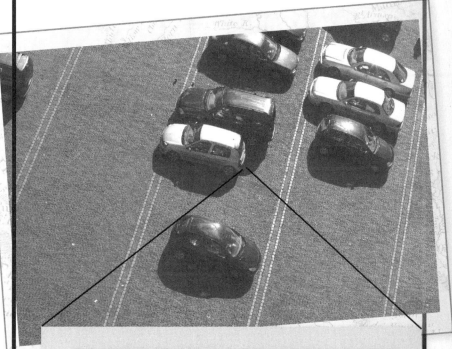

AS LONG AS THERE ARE TESTS, THERE WILL BE PRAYER IN PUBLIC SCHOOLS.

People who don't say "thanks" for a road courtesy.

Drivers who play music so loud that it vibrates your car.

"Any man who can drive safely while kissing a pretty girl is simply not giving the kiss the attention it deserves." — Albert Einstein

SOMETIMES I WAKE UP GRUMPY, SOMETIMES I LET HER SLEEP.

29

The lone driver in the carpool lane.

Send the Money
A man once answered an advertisement in the newspaper, which said, "New Porsche — $50." After paying for the car, he asked why the woman had sold it at such a low price. She said, "My husband ran off with his secretary, and sent me a telegram saying, 'Sell the Porsche and send me the money.'"

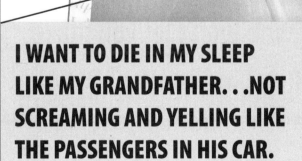

I WANT TO DIE IN MY SLEEP LIKE MY GRANDFATHER. . .NOT SCREAMING AND YELLING LIKE THE PASSENGERS IN HIS CAR.

Cars in front of you with loose loads.

Drivers who won't let you make eye contact as they wait to get onto the road from a driveway.

IT'S AS *BAD* AS YOU THINK, AND THEY *ARE* OUT TO GET YOU.

Drivers who pretend they haven't seen you as they steal your parking space.

OKAY, WHO STOPPED THE PAYMENT ON MY REALITY CHECK?

"A driver is a king on a vinyl bucket-seat throne, changing direction with the turn of a wheel, changing the climate with a flick of the button, changing the music with the switch of a dial."
— Andrew H. Malcolm

Drivers who move at two mph up to a green light, make it through the yellow, and leave you with a red light.

Motorists who throw trash out of their car windows.

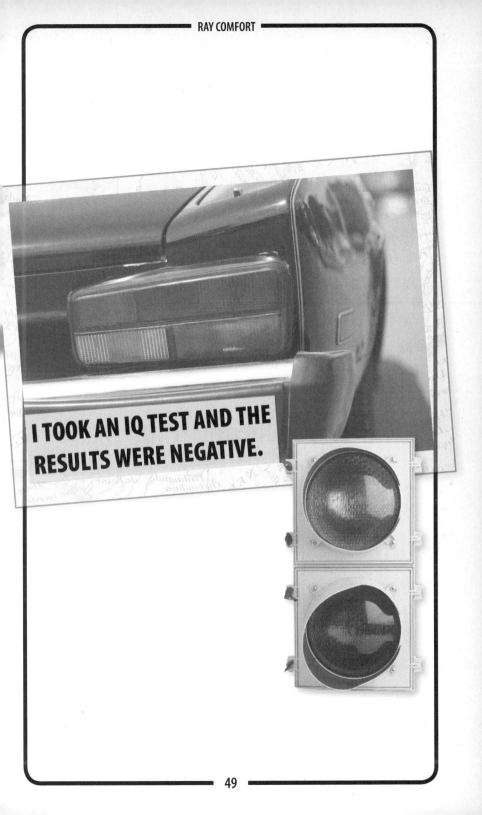

I TOOK AN IQ TEST AND THE RESULTS WERE NEGATIVE.

35

Drivers who drive onto the shoulder to get ahead of a line of traffic.

Bank Robbers and Burglars

In Houston, Texas, police set out with their sirens wailing after three bank robbers who had merged into freeway traffic. Unbeknown to the police, two burglars who had just pulled a job were also on the freeway, and took off at high speed, mistakenly thinking that the law was chasing them. The police immediately did give chase . . . and apprehended the men after they crashed their car in panic.

PARDON MY DRIVING, I'M RELOADING.

36

Drivers who refuse to go fast enough to pass a police car, no matter how slow it is going.

37

Motorcyclists that speed between lanes of stationary traffic at 600 mph.

I BRAKE FOR TAILGATERS.

Drivers who indicate that they
are about to change lanes,
but take 15 miles to do so.

HONK IF YOU LOVE PEACE AND QUIET.

Judge for Yourself

In Rolling Meadows, Illinois, a Cook County correctional officer named Michael Moreci was put under investigation and faced a fine of up to $500 for yelling, *"I beat up guys like you for a living!"* to a motorist. The motorist he yelled at was Judge Sam Amirante.

Trucks that signal to
change lanes and then
come over, ready or not.

Drivers who block traffic
for an hour while waiting
for a parking spot.

NOTHING IS FOOLPROOF TO A SUFFICIENTLY TALENTED FOOL.

41

Drivers who park on parking lines, taking up as many spots as possible.

ON THE OTHER HAND, YOU HAVE DIFFERENT FINGERS.

"When buying a used car, punch the buttons on the radio. If all the stations are rock and roll, there's a good chance the transmission is shot." — Larry Lujack

Drivers who park so close to your car, you can't open your door to get in.

Drivers who drive through parking lots at 80 mph.

IF YOU CAN READ THIS, YOU ARE TOO CLOSE!

44

The driver who parks his car in the middle of the road to drop off 38 relatives.

I DON'T FIND IT HARD TO MEET EXPENSES. THEY'RE EVERYWHERE.

Blowing It

Man has a talent when it comes to blowing it. Take for example the experience of an Englishman named Mr. Peter Rolands. When he found himself in conditions so freezing that he couldn't get his key into the lock of his vehicle, he decided to use some ingenuity by blowing warm air into the lock. Unfortunately, his lips touched the freezing metal and locked to it.

As he knelt beside the door of his car, held fast with his lips on the lock, an elderly woman stopped and inquired as to whether or not Mr. Rolands was okay. The poor man responded with, "Alra? Itmmlgptk!!!" at which the woman became frightened and ran away.

He was trapped in that posture for 20 minutes, until continual hot breathing loosed his chilled lips.

Bus drivers you let go in front of you, who leave you with a cloud of diesel smoke in appreciation.

Drivers that attempt to pass you when you stop for a pedestrian.

I JUST LET MY MIND WANDER,
AND IT DIDN'T COME BACK.

Drivers who leave
their shopping carts in
parking spaces.

"Car sickness is the feeling you get when the monthly payment is due." — Author Unknown

IF YOU DON'T LIKE MY DRIVING, STAY OFF THE SIDEWALK.

Drivers who empty ashtrays on the ground in shopping center parking lots.

Drivers who signal *after* they change lanes.

ALL GENERALIZATIONS ARE FALSE.

Drivers who signal
as they approach a
curve in the road.

Feeling Run Down

If you have a few problems, the following incident, which was published in the *Reader's Digest*, should bring things into perspective.

In July of 1988, a 49-year-old rancher in Idaho was dismounting his still running tractor when he stood on a gob of grease. As he slid, he grabbed the control bar for support. This put the tractor in gear. It lunged forward and he was thrown off balance, hitting the throttle lever. He then fell to the ground in front of the wheel of the now moving tractor. Unfortunately, he had filled the 18" wide tires with water to give it more traction. It worked. As the 9,600-pound tractor ran over his body he felt his pelvic bones breaking. The tractor then drove over his chest breaking ribs as it did so, just missing his head.

As the farmer lay in the dirt, his only consoling thought was the fact that the tractor would hit the fence and alert his neighbors that something was wrong. Not so. It hit a hay bale, jerking the front wheels to one side, did a complete circle around the field and came for him a second time. As it headed for him, he mustered all his energy and rolled his shattered body out of its path. Safe! Nope. It hit an oil can, turning its front wheels to one side *and it came around the field again!* This time it ran over his legs!

The unfortunate man was found some time later, and lived to face a $40,000 medical bill.

IT'S BEEN MONDAY ALL WEEK.

Drivers who signal to turn left, then turn right.

Drivers who indicate that they are about to turn 150 miles before they actually do.

WORK IS FOR PEOPLE WHO DON'T KNOW HOW TO FISH.

"The only aspect of our travels that is interesting to others is disaster." — *Martha Gellman*

Drivers who use their signals to show you that they will be turning in 3/10 of a second.

Save the Whales

In Oregon, some clever authorities decided that they would blow up a beached dead whale with dynamite, rather than go to the trouble and expense of burying the rotting mammal. They surmised that after it was blown up, the hundreds of hungry seagulls that were hanging around would then eat the small portions of the big fish and deal with the problem. The crowds and news media were moved back one-fourth of a mile and the dynamite was exploded.

Unfortunately, thousands of pieces of rotten whale landed on the crowd, with one big whale portion landing on a spectator's car, denting the roof in about 18 inches. The noise of the explosion caused the birds to completely disappear, leaving authorities with the exciting job of picking up the thousands of pieces of stinking whale and burying them.

I BRAKE FOR NO APPARENT REASON.

Drivers who pull out in front of oncoming traffic.

Drivers who forget to turn off their signals

I WONDER HOW MUCH DEEPER THE OCEAN WOULD BE WITHOUT SPONGES.

56

Oncoming drivers who stray over to your side of the road because there is no center divider.

I USED TO THINK I WAS TOO INDECISIVE, BUT NOW I'M NOT TOO SURE.

"The one thing that unites all human beings, regardless of age, gender, religion, economic status, or ethnic background, is that, deep down inside, we ALL believe that we are above average drivers." — Dave Barry, Things That It Took Me 50 Years to Learn

Drivers who swing open their door into oncoming traffic.

Oncoming drivers who read maps while driving.

I CAN HANDLE PAIN UNTIL IT HURTS.

59

Drivers who drive with six dogs on their lap.

IF EVERYTHING IS COMING YOUR WAY, THEN YOU'RE IN THE WRONG LANE.

A Screw Loose

When my daughter's car cassette radio wasn't working I quickly offered to fix it. She had hit a bump on the freeway and it had stopped playing, so it was simply a matter of reattaching a loose wire.

I opened the car door and skillfully ran my hand under the dashboard, but couldn't feel anything, so I decided that I needed to *see* what I was doing. I'm not stupid — if I blindly poke my fingers around wires, I could be shocked. The trouble was that the area was so confined that the only way I could see under the dashboard was to maneuver myself upside-down across the passenger seat, similar to the way a high jumper goes over a bar.

It was a brilliant move. In that position I could see all the way along the underside of the dash. I had turned the motor on so that the cassette would play if I attached the right wire. Intelligent, huh? Problem. *There weren't any wires* — it was all internal. It was then that I decided that I had better maneuver myself out, and discovered an interesting thing. An upside-down human body with its head near a car floor, its back on the seat, and its feet sticking out the door can't move at all.

Drivers who try and get into their car with ½" between them and oncoming traffic.

Drivers who, when making a left turn, stay as far to the right as possible.

"The shortest distance between two points is under construction."
— *Noelie Altito*

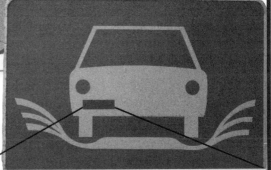

**THE MORE PEOPLE I MEET,
THE MORE I LIKE MY DOG.**

62

Oncoming drivers who hug the middle line.

THIS STATEMENT IS FALSE.

"It is impossible to travel faster than the speed of light, and certainly not desirable, as one's hat keeps blowing off." — Woody Allen

Drivers who cut corners.

Drivers whose rear window reflects the sun in your eyes.

THEY TOLD ME I WAS GUILLIBLE...
AND I BELIEVED THEM.

The Tired Lady

A woman became tired at Venice Beach, California in the summer of 1994. The police beach patrol vehicle ran over her as she lay face down in the sand, about 50 feet from the water's edge. The woman, who was impressed with the vehicle they were driving, was treated at a local hospital and discharged the same day.

The driver who walks to his car in a parking lot in the middle of the road so that cars have to drive at one mph behind him.

Calling Card

A criminal recently broke into a warehouse and carried items out of the back door to his get-away vehicle. After the theft had been discovered, police found that the robber had held the back door open with a folded piece of paper. When they unfolded it, they discovered that it was a traffic ticket that had been issued to the man that morning, complete with this name, address, and license plate number.

IT'S BAD LUCK TO BE SUPERSTITIOUS.

Drivers who veer to the left just before they make a right turn.

The revving maniac.

ACCORDING TO MY BEST RECOLLECTION, I DON'T REMEMBER.

Drivers who suddenly back
up when they realize they
have made a wrong turn.

"A real patriot is the fellow who gets a parking ticket and rejoices that the system works."
— *Bill Vaughan*

CONSIDER: AMATEURS BUILT THE ARK. PROFESSIONALS BUILT THE TITANIC.

Drivers who stop behind you close enough to count your nasal hair in your rearview mirror.

Drivers who suddenly go blind when the light turns green.

GRAVITY ALWAYS GETS ME DOWN.

"I never travel without my diary. One should always have something sensational to read in the train."
— *Oscar Wilde*

Drivers who park in front
of the drive-through
mailbox at a post office,
leaving their car in a red
zone to buy stamps.

DESPITE THE COST OF LIVING, HAVE YOU NOTICED HOW IT REMAINS SO POPULAR?

"The elderly don't drive that badly; they're just the only ones with time to do the speed limit." — Jason Love

Speeders who speed up to a
stop light, trusting your life
to their brakes.

Drivers who slow down
to a snail's pace because
they see a red light two
miles ahead of them.

A DAY WITHOUT SUNSHINE
IS LIKE NIGHT.

Drivers who follow a car that has just run a red light.

Hot Car

In the late seventies, I ran a "Drug Prevention Center" which was located on "High" street, which is an unfortunate choice of street names for a drug prevention center.

One day, I answered the telephone to hear that a member of our drug team had failed to show up at a school to do a talk. I said that I would get there as soon as possible and do it myself. Someone in the center threw her keys at me and said, "Take my car. It's a Volkswagen on the third floor of the parking building." I caught the keys, ran up to the third floor, jumped in the car, and drove to the school. An hour later, I returned to the building, parked the car, and went back to the center.

As I walked in, I threw the keys back and casually said, "What are you doing with a Radio Avon sticker on your car? That's a secular station." She looked curiously at me and said, "*I don't have a Radio Avon sticker on my car!*"

We both ran back to the third floor of the parking building. Sure enough, the keys had fit, and I had taken someone else's car and driven around town for an hour!

CORDUROY PILLOWS: THEY'RE MAKING HEADLINES!

The driver who stops dead in the road, and doesn't let you know what he is about to do.

Drivers who stop at lights, then stick the front of their car into an intersection and refuse to pull back even slightly.

"Another way to solve the traffic problems of this country is to pass a law that only paid-for cars be allowed to use the highways." — Will Rogers

GRAVITY — IT'S NOT JUST A GOOD IDEA, ITS THE *LAW*!

The ice cream truck driver who plays "Home on the Range" every day for 100 years.

LIFE IS TOO COMPLICATED IN THE MORNING.

"A good traveler has no fixed plans and is not intent on arriving." — Lao Tzu

78

Drivers who remain stationary when you gesture them to go, then pull out at the same time as you.

79

Drivers who honk if you don't pull out within two microseconds of the light turning green.

Drivers who wait at an intersection until you are 50 feet in front of them before they pull out.

ASK ME ABOUT MY VOW OF SILENCE.

Honking Hubby

A man had a habit of honking his horn each day as he came home from work. His loving and faithful wife would immediately, upon hearing the honk, open the garage door. He would swing around a sharp corner and drive straight into the already-opened garage.

His wife was consistent in her door-opening ministry, until one day she failed to hear the car horn. Her happy honking husband swung around the sharp corner, up the driveway, through the closed doors, through the back wall, and into the vegetable garden.

People who honk at you to turn right on a red, when a sign says, "No turn on red."

Drivers who don't take their turn at four-way stops.

I'M NOT DRIVING FAST — JUST FLYING LOW.

83

Drivers who do illegal U-turns.

DIPLOMACY IS THE ART OF LETTING SOMEONE ELSE GET YOUR WAY.

"Two wrongs don't make a right, but three lefts do."
— *Jason Love*

Drivers who never turn
right on a red light.

Drivers who park in front of your
driveway because they have
seen a yard sale in your street.

IF IGNORANCE IS BLISS, THEN TOURISTS ARE IN A CONSTANT STATE OF EUPHORIA.

Double-parked drivers who block the road while chatting to a friend.

"Only he who has traveled the road knows where the potholes are deep." — *Chinese Proverb*

NO MATTER WHERE YOU GO, YOU'RE THERE.

Drivers who won't let you cross lanes to get to a certain freeway.

Two truck drivers who play concertina with your vehicle.

I INTEND TO LIVE FOREVER
— SO FAR, SO GOOD.

A Mind of Its Own

A police officer in Nebraska left his vehicle running in "drive" after pulling over a truck for inspection. It sat stationary for three minutes until the air conditioner automatically switched off, releasing more power to the motor. It then drove itself forward, right into the back of the truck he was inspecting.

The officer had just installed a video system into his vehicle, which is now used to train officers on what not to do.

Drivers who try and
beat the train by driving
around arm barriers.

The Winner

In West Virginia, a man won a game of "chicken" with a train. The 22 year old and a friend were seeing who could stay on the track longest as the train sped toward them. He beat his friend, but was hit by the train and tossed nearly 70 feet. He was taken to a hospital where he was listed as being in serious condition.

WHAT HAPPENS IF YOU GET SCARED HALF TO DEATH TWICE?

Drivers who go against the arrows in parking lots.

Oncoming drivers who refuse to take their lights off high beam.

"Walking isn't a lost art — one must, by some means, get to the garage." — Evan Esar

I USED TO HAVE AN OPEN MIND BUT MY BRAINS KEPT FALLING OUT.

The driver who starts his car
at 3:00 a.m. on cold mornings,
and warms it up by leaving it
running for five hours before
he goes to work.

ENERGIZER BUNNY ARRESTED, CHARGED WITH BATTERY.

Patience is something you admire in the driver behind you and scorn in the one ahead.
— Mac McCleary

Drivers who wait until the early hours of the morning to cover your street with rubber from their tires.

Drivers who insist on merging in front of you, when there is a huge gap behind you.

I'VE HAD AMNESIA AS LONG
AS I CAN REMEMBER.

95

Drivers in front of you who travel too close.

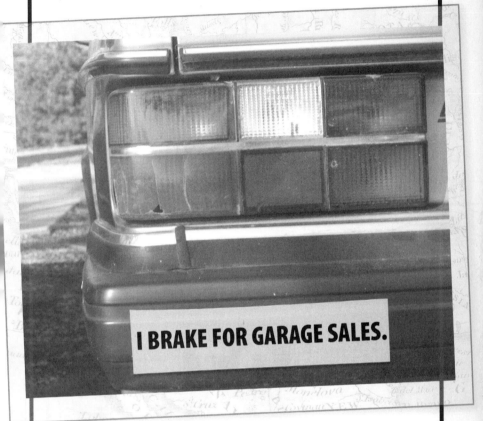

"On the other hand, the Bible contains much that is relevant today, like Noah taking 40 days to find a place to park." — Curtis McDougall

Drivers whose children stare at you as their car passes yours.

Drivers who slam on their brakes for things like bees, moths, and flies.

VACATION BEGINS WHEN DAD SAYS, "I KNOW A SHORT CUT."

98

Drivers who can't stay in their lane, even when sober.

WHAT'S ANOTHER WORD FOR THESAURUS?

Big-Bang Theory

When a man's vehicle broke down on a highway, a woman pulled alongside him and asked if she could push-start his car with her car. He said that his vehicle was an automatic and therefore needed to be pushed at 35 mph before it would start. The woman nodded, turned her car around and drove back down the street. She then did a U turn and hit the man's car . . . at 35 mph!

Drivers whose cars have bumper stickers from 100-year-old presidential races.

Drivers who insist on having two-foot square dice, novelty footballs, kitchen sinks, and other view-restricting paraphernalia hanging from their rearview mirror.

EVERYWHERE IS WALKING DISTANCE IF YOU HAVE THE TIME.

Drivers who write books
about annoying things
other drivers do.

"A suburban mother's role is to deliver children
obstetrically once, and by car forever after."
— Peter De Vries

**I WENT TO THE FIGHTS, AND A
HOCKEY GAME BROKE OUT.**

Beware of Trees

Here's a question for you: What is the greater killer of drivers in the United States? Perhaps you think it's drunk drivers, or maybe head-on collisions, heart attacks, or falling asleep at the wheel. But it's none of these. The greatest killer of drivers in the United States is trees. Trees were merely pleasant decorations on the side of the road during the horse and buggy era, but as the motorcar evolved, they became the silent killer of multitudes. Every year, a total of 40,000 people in the United States die while driving. That's a sobering thought. However, if you are like me, you have the attitude that sudden death is something that happens to other people. I am sure that if we could speak to each of those 40,000 who are now dead, they would say, "I never thought that it would happen to me." We may be careful, and even prayerful, but in the light of so many deaths, driving in modern America is fatefully dangerous.

So what can you do to save yourself from such a terrible death? Here are six sensible thoughts to keep you alive:

1. Always buckle up.
2. Never drink and drive.
3. Slow down in the rain.
4. Travel at a safe distance from the car in front of you.
5. Never drive when you are tired.
6. Drive with the knowledge that you are fallible — you have the potential to take someone else's life as well as your own.

I consider myself to be a good driver. However, I know that I am guilty of doing things that have annoyed other drivers — and I have probably ignorantly done a number of other things to upset other drivers. Life is very similar. Years ago, if you asked me if I was a good person, I would have said that I was. I would have said, "If there is a heaven, I will probably make it because I'm not a bad person." But I was making a terrible mistake. God has a list of ten things we must do — they are called the Ten Commandments. In my ignorance, I didn't realize that I had already broken those Commandments and was in great danger.

The biblical explanation as to why each of us will die is because we have broken an uncompromising law. Just as we suffer the consequences of breaking the law of gravity if we step off a ten-story building, so we will suffer the consequences of transgressing God's Moral Law. Let's see if you have broken this Law (commonly referred to as the Ten Commandments):

1. Is God first in your life? Do you love Him with all of your heart, mind, soul, and strength? Do you love your neighbor as yourself? Does your love for your family seem like hatred compared to the love you have for the One who gave those loved ones to you?

2. Have you made a god in your own image, to suit yourself?

3. Have you ever used God's holy name in vain . . . substituting it for a four-lettered filth word to express disgust?

4. Have you kept the Sabbath holy?

5. Have you always honored your parents?

6. Have you hated anyone? Then the Bible says you are a murderer.

7. Have you had sex before marriage? Or have you lusted after another person? The Bible warns that you have committed adultery in your heart.

8. Have you ever stolen something? Then you are a thief.

9. If you have told even one lie, you are a liar and cannot enter the kingdom of God.

10. Finally, have you ever desired something that belonged to someone else? Then you have broken the Tenth Commandment.

Listen to your conscience. The Law leaves us *all* sinners in God's sight. On Judgment Day we will be found guilty and end up in hell forever. Perhaps you are sorry for your sins, and you even confess them to God, but that doesn't mean that He will forgive you — no matter how sincere you are. Let me explain why. Imagine you are standing guilty in front of a judge. You face a $50,000 fine, and say, "Judge . . . I'm truly sorry for my crime." He would probably say, "So you should be! Now are you able to pay the $50,000 fine or not?" A judge must have *grounds* upon which he can release you. If I paid your fine, *then* you would be free from the demands of the law.

That's precisely what God did in the person of Jesus Christ. Each of us stands guilty of breaking God's Law, but because Jesus paid our fine on the Cross 2,000 years ago, God can forgive us on the grounds of His suffering death. That's why you need Jesus Christ as your Savior. Without Him, the Law will send you to hell, and you will have no one to blame but yourself. God will make sure justice is carried out. The Bible says, "God commends His love toward us in that while we were yet sinners Christ died for us" (Rom. 5:8; NKJV). He gave His sinless life on the Cross, showing the depth of God's love for us. We broke God's Law — He paid the fine so that we could be free from its perfect demands. Then He rose from the dead and defeated the power of the grave.

If you repent, trust in the Savior, and obey His Word, God will forgive your sins and grant you everlasting life. The Bible says that all humanity is held captive to the fear of and power of death (Heb. 2:15). If you don't face your fear of death, then you will run from it until the day you die . . . and that day *will* come. The proof of your sin will be your death. Today, not only face the reality that you will die, *but also do something about it* — obey the gospel and live. Confess your sins to God, put your faith in Jesus Christ, then read the Bible daily and obey what you read. God will never let you down. For more information go to www.livingwaters.com and click on "Save Yourself Some Pain."

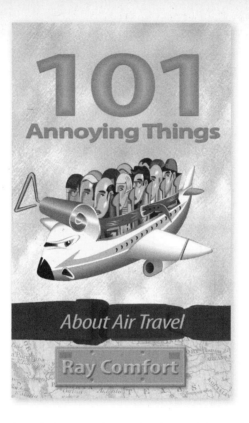

Do you know the frustration of arriving three hours early for your flight, only to find when you arrive that it has been delayed? Have you suffered at the hands of baggage handlers who think your luggage is a punching bag? Evangelist Ray Comfort shares how to turn frustrations into evangelism opportunities.

• *Lost baggage: God finds you where you are*
• *Oversold flights: There's always room for one more*
• *Mindbenders, funny quotes, jokes, riddles, and more*

Well-known apologist and evangelist Comfort has come up with over a hundred amusing encounters and annoying things about air travel experienced throughout his extensive travels. No more than two paragraphs each, each entry also includes a joke or a riddle.

Designed as an evangelizing tool, the book also includes a salvation message. These comical experiences endured by almost everyone in the course of traveling culminate in a firm presentation of the gospel.

ISBN: 0-89221-669-7 • ISBN 13: 978-0-89221-669-7
176 pages • 5 1/4 x 8 3/8 • Trade Paper • Retail: $10.99
HUMOR / General

JUN 18 2007